IT'S REALLY HARD
TRYING TO BE ME

IT'S REALLY HARD
TRYING TO BE ME

WRITTEN BY
AMY BALDWIN RUSSELL

ILLUSTRATED BY
SOPHISTICATED PRESS

Copyright © 2024 by Amy Russell

ISBN 979-8-218-52805-8

All rights reserved. No part of this publication may be reproduced, distributed, or transmitted in any form or by any means, including photocopying, recording, or other electronic or mechanical methods, without the prior written permission of the publisher, except in the case of brief quotations embodied in critical reviews and certain other noncommercial uses permitted by copyright law. For permission requests, write to the publisher, addressed

Ordering Information: Quantity sales. Special discounts are available on quantity purchases by corporations, associations, and others. For details, contact the publisher at the email address above. Orders by U.S. trade bookstores and wholesalers.

Please contact Amy Russell: abrauthor65@gmail.co

Printed in the United States of America

Publisher: Amy Russell

Publisher Consultant

Do your parents give you a choice? Do your parents have lots of rules? Do they let you have a voice? Do they let you do some of the things that you want to do?

Do your parents let you be you?

Rules!
Rules!
Rules!

It is interesting how parents tell you to be yourself and not be like everyone else. Then, they won't let you make any decisions. They won't let you have a voice. They make all the decisions for you. They won't even give you a choice.

I want choices!
I want to have a voice.!"

My parents make me get my hair cut. They won't let me wear my hair long. Why do I have to get a haircut? Having long hair isn't wrong. Why can't I just be me? I like being me.

My dad preaches about being like Jesus. Jesus had long hair. Nobody made him get his hair cut. I want to be like Jesus. This really isn't fair. Can I have a second opinion? God, please answer my prayer. I'm just trying to be me.

My parents tell me to make my bed. They tell me to clean my room. Isn't that what everybody does? I feel like I'm doomed. Why can't my room be messy? Why does it have to be clean? Having my room cleaned is my mom's and dad's house cleaning dream. Why can't I just be me?

HELLO

When my friends come over to play, my parents won't let them stay very long. After we have played for a while, my parents say that we have played long enough. Now it is time for them to go home. I want them to stay longer. I don't want them to go. I ask if they can stay a little longer, but my parents say "no."
Will my parents ever let me be me?

My parents make me tuck in my shirt, even when I am not at church or school. Why does my shirt have to be tucked in all the time. My parents have way too many rules. I wish they would let me be me.

"Please let me be me".

My parents make me go to church every Sunday and wear church clothes too. Do your parents treat you this way? What about you? I don't ever get a break. Why can't I wear regular clothes to church? I don't know how much more I can take.

I just want them to let me be me.

I want to get cornrows in my hair. Of course, my parents say no. "They say "cornrows are not for you". "We've told you this before"! They won't let me have my own style. Why can't I have my own flow?
I'm just trying to be me.

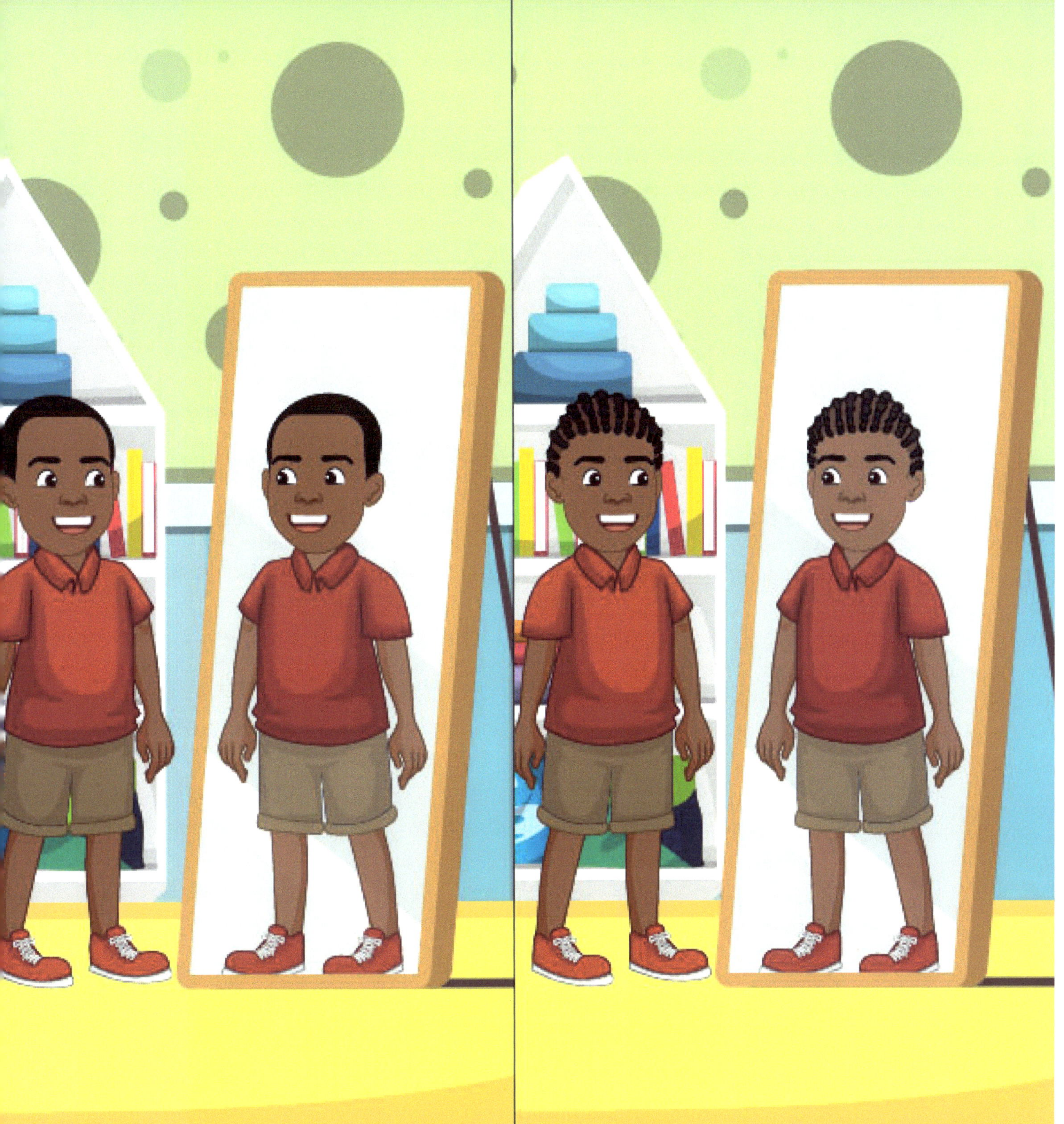

I like to eat pizza, hotdogs, and hamburgers too. My parents make me eat things like beans, greens, broccoli, and beef stew. They won't let me eat what I want to eat. They will not let me be me.

YES
NO

I want to stay up late, watch TV, and play
video games sometimes.
I'm not into it very deep. My parents make me
go to bed early.
They say, "you have to go to school in the morning".
"You need to get your sleep. I'm just trying
to have a little fun.
I'm just trying to be me.

1:15 A.M

I want to ride the bus to school, but my parents say no. My mom teaches at my school. She won't let me ride the bus. She says, "you don't need to ride the bus when I drive every day". I just want to ride with my friends. What more can a fellow say? I just want my parents to let me be me.

SCHOOL BUS

They make me do my homework or study every night. I don't mind doing my homework if it doesn't take too long. My mom checks it closely. She sings the same old song. "This isn't right". "You need to do it again." She makes me write with a pencil, but I want to write with my pen. I just want to be me.

When I play basketball, they make me give it all I've got. Well, I'm pretty good at basketball, but Michael Jordan, I am not. I just want to play the game. Timothy Russell is my name. I am trying hard to just be me.

When we order from McDonalds, they order me a Happy Meal. That child burger and fry are simply not enough. It's not a good deal. I want the toy, but a quarter-pounder with a large fry instead. I'm a growing boy. I'm just trying to get fed. This is part of who I am. This is me being me!

SELF
ORDERING
BIG BURGER
BURGER
Burger
happy

When it's time to buy new shoes, I want a pair of Jordan's. My mom says, "no, I can buy five pairs of shoes for just that one price." Now, I hope that my dad will let me have a pair. I hope that my dad will be nice. He's not as cheap as my mom. My dad is a little cooler, you see. I just want to wear Jordans. I'm just trying to be me.

My parents make me say my prayers every night before I go to bed, but some nights I don't feel like praying. I just want to go to sleep instead. They teach me the Lord's Prayer by repeating every word they say. They teach me to be thankful for every single day. I know that praying every night is the right thing to do, but by bedtime, I am very tired and terribly sleepy, too. My parents don't have a clue. I just want to be me.

I say to my dad, "I'm old enough to make some decisions on my own." My dad says to me, "You need to enjoy being a kid while you still can." You have plenty of time to grow up and become a man."

My mom signed me up for piano lessons, but I want to play the drums. They compromise with me. I end up playing both and the progress begins. I feel like they're beginning to understand me a little. I feel like I 'm beginning to win. My parents are starting to listen to me as you can clearly see. Maybe they are ready to start letting me be me.

Although my parents have many rules and control almost everything I do, I think they're trying to teach me about life, protect me, and care for me, too. With my parents' love and guidance, which really is the key, I am beginning to understand. I think I'm beginning to see. For these reasons, I will be the best me that I can possibly be.

"I'm going to be the best me I can be."
HELLO

The End

About The Autor

Amy Baldwin Russell is a wife, daughter, mother, and grandmother. She was born and raised in Chatom, Alabama. Growing up there, she actively participated in her community, school, and the local church. It was in Chatom, AL that Amy developed her faith, strength, courage, and determination to face life's challenges and not accept the ordinary as a way of life.

Amy has had a love for words, writing, and education since her pre-elementary years. She recalls being able to sound out and pronounce words as early as 4 years old with the support and encouragement of her parents, especially her father. She has always been intrigued with words, rhyme, and rhythm. She has been a passionate elementary educator for the past 30 years, which has also been instrumental in her desire to write and publish children's books.

Amy holds an AS degree in General Education from Bishop State College in Mobile, AL, and a BS degree in Early Childhood Education from Shorter College in Rome, GA. She is gifted and talented endorsed as well. Amy holds a MA in Curriculum and Instruction from Grand Canyon University in Phoenix Arizona.

Amy considers her faith in God and her family to be essential elements in her life. She has a love and passion for singing, writing, fishing, traveling, spending time with her family, and serving God.

You can contact Amy for booking by visiting abrauthor65@gmail.com

www.ingramcontent.com/pod-product-compliance
Lightning Source LLC
Chambersburg PA
CBHW042051110726
48006CB00002B/354